HAPPINESS *for* EVERYONE

applying a Universal Happiness Formula
to the four sources of Happiness

ALSO AVAILABLE FROM HANS BEUMER:

THE GLOBAL TRAVELLER SERIES

KUMANO KODO
20'000 KM BY TRAIN

THE ULTIMATE HAPPINESS SERIES

TRAVEL GUIDE TO SELF-ACTUALIZATION

Visit www.hansbeumer.com

THE ULTIMATE HAPPINESS SERIES

HAPPINESS *for* EVERYONE

applying a Universal Happiness Formula
to the four sources of Happiness

HANS BEUMER

Hans Beumer Publications
2016

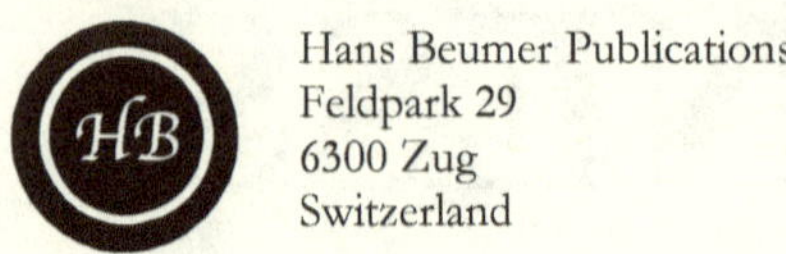

Hans Beumer Publications
Feldpark 29
6300 Zug
Switzerland

Text Copyright © Hans Beumer 2016
Equations Copyright © Hans Beumer 2016
Tables and Graphs Copyright © Hans Beumer 2016
Cover Icons designed by Freepik from www.flaticon.com

All rights reserved. No part of this book may be reproduced by any mechanical, photographic, or electronic process, or in the form of a phonographic recording, nor may it be stored in a retrieval system, transmitted, or otherwise be copied for public or private use without the express written permission of the publisher, except for the use of brief quotations in a book review.

First edition published in June 2016:

This book is available as:
-Paperback (B/W): ISBN 978-3-906861-09-8
-EBook: ISBN 978-3-906861-10-4

Typeset body text in Garamond 11.5
Printed and distributed by Lulu Press, Inc.

www.hansbeumer.com

This book is not intended to provide personalised health, financial, emotional or spiritual advice. It provides the viewpoints of the Author, but the views expressed should not be taken as expert instructions or commands. The reader is responsible for his or her own decisions and actions and when in need for health advice should consult their physician, for financial advice should consult their financial advisor, and for emotional and spiritual advice consult whomever they entrust these topics with. The Author and Publisher specifically disclaim any liability, loss, damage, or risk, personal or otherwise, that is incurred as a consequence, directly or indirectly, of the use and application of any of the contents of this book.

CONTENTS

FOREWORD

Do you know that you already possess everything you need to be happy within you? Do you know that therefore everyone can be happy, irrespective of their current circumstances, level of income and health?

Many other books cover the topic of happiness, be it from a scientific, neurological, religious, spiritual or universal perspective, and use difficult and technical language on many hundreds of pages of lengthy texts. *Happiness for Everyone* remarkably differs from all these other books. It is concise and to the point and through the use of the Happiness Portfolio, it provides an analytical, structured and simple to understand guide to your personal happiness. The Happiness Portfolio captures this on one page in a simple visualisation, which can serve as your life's guide to enduring happiness.

The Happiness Portfolio, when followed, has the intense power to achieve happiness for everybody, everywhere, anytime. As with achieving any goal in your life, of course, this needs clarity, courage, determination, and persistence. But when you follow through, happiness will surely come to you, with the certainty of the outcome of a mathematical formula.

For this purpose, I combined ancient and philosophical wisdom about happiness in a Universal Happiness Formula. Apply this formula to the main aspects of your life, capture the results in your Happiness Portfolio, and happiness is a sure outcome.

I hope that this book inspires you to pursue and find your happiness, so that you soon reach your Ultimate Happiness level.

Read to advance your life,
drs. Hans Beumer
June 2016

Chapter 1

THE UNIVERSAL HAPPINESS FORMULA

What is Happiness?

From a biological point of view, happiness is a personal feeling of positive emotions created by the release of certain chemicals in the brain. Dopamine is released in the brain when you are seeking the feelings of rewards from setting and achieving goals, and triggers curiosity, expectation, anticipation, excitement, learning and desire, promoting advancement of your personal life. The brain releases Oxytocin when you are close with another person, when you have an intimate relationship, when you are bonding with another person, promoting social behaviour in your personal life. Endorphins kill pain, and are produced during (exhausting) physical exercise and sexual activity, to promote endurance in your personal life. The Serotonin chemical is responsible for controlling your mood. The brain increases the levels of Serotonin when you are pursuing things that increase the sense of purpose and achievement in your personal life. The majority of Serotonin is produced in the intestines, and is directly influenced by the state of hunger. If you are hungry, you are likely going to be in a bad mood.
These chemicals are released in the brain based on certain trigger events and these releases are not in an enduring, permanent, flow but only temporary. Brain-chemically, they can't be sustained permanently. That is why the highly elated emotions of happiness usually last relatively short.

From an evolutionary point of view, feelings of happiness and pleasure are nothing else than an incentive system promoting the repetition of behaviour which is beneficial for the survival of the species. That is why sex, intended for procreation, generates such feelings of pleasure, excitement and ecstasy. That is why we enjoy eating chocolate, deserts, candy, donuts, and other sweets. High calorie foods gave the early humans high energy for surviving in harsh climates with monotone menus. That is why we enjoy the interaction with other human beings, as during the early times of the human species, such interaction between humans was needed to survive in a dangerous and hostile world (a lone early human would not be able to survive outside the social group).

Each of the above mentioned chemicals also have a counterpart, chemicals that bring a person in an unhappy state. Nature's intention is that these chemicals trigger actions that remove the unpleasantness and unhappiness. Evolution has designed our protection system in such a way that it prevents the human species (and other species as well) to continue to do things which may endanger the survival of the body. It is in the body's best interest that pain, hunger and other unpleasant feelings are eliminated as quickly as possible.

It is nature and the evolution that have developed the positive and negative chemicals that are released in the brain when certain triggers are set off. Therefore, we humans have an evolutionary condition which makes us strive for happiness and limit suffering. Nature's protection mechanism makes us experience unpleasant feelings more intensely than pleasant feelings, as unpleasant feelings signal immediate dangers for survival of the individual organism, deserving all attention. It is to prevent repetitive negative behaviour. This answers the question why not everybody has the courage to take risks in achieving happiness (e.g. by leaving the comfort zone of an existing job, even when unhappy, in search for a job where one is passionate about), but rather succumb to a mediocre or unhappy life. It is nature's protection mechanism at work, where the desire for a happy life is overshadowed by the risk-aversion, as a change could also lead to something worse instead of something better.

These evolutionary conditions make us strive for happiness and limit unhappiness. That is why each of the 7.5 billion people on Earth is on their personal happiness quest. This is the only true answer to the question why we humans are always in search for happiness. We are all simply programmed this way.

The Baseline Coefficient

Don't we all know someone who is always complaining, who is never satisfied with what he or she has or receives? The glass is always half empty? A person who always focuses on the negative things? No matter what life gives this person, they will never be really happy for a longer time. Then you probably also know someone who always radiates, focuses on the positive things, appreciates even the smallest gestures, sees the glass as half full, etc. In other words, each person has their inherent level of baseline happiness.

The baseline coefficient represents an adjustment in the Happiness Equation, correcting the level for the happiness baseline of a person. The Baseline Coefficient is a constant quantity in the equation. In case a person's baseline coefficient is 5 (for example out of a maximum level of 10), that person has a level of happiness which is more or less neutral, not unhappy, but a level of general contentment.
In case a person has a baseline coefficient between 0 and 5 (out of the 10), their inherent happiness feeling will be low, rather, they will feel unhappy and dissatisfied with their life, regardless of how their life develops.
In case the baseline coefficient is between 5 and 10 (out of the 10), that person has a positive mindset, will generally feel happy with their life, and put a positive spin on the events in their life.

The relative level of a person's baseline influences the Happiness Equation as follows:

Consideration of Baseline Coefficient: Happiness = Fixed Baseline Coefficient + Variable Other Factors Weights: 100% = 40% + 60%

There are only few studies on this topic, concluding that the baseline can make up to 50% of the influence on happiness. For the purpose of this book, I set the weight at 40% for the Fixed Baseline Coefficient, and at 60% for other variable factors.

In the long run the baseline is fixed for a person, despite what happens to that person. For example, if a person becomes disabled, in the first period there will be a significant drop in happiness, far below the baseline level. But it appears that after some time, the person gets used to their disability, learns to live with it, and gradually the happiness level returns to the same baseline as before the disability. In case such baseline was high, the person will make the most out of their new situation and continue to expand on their life by fuelling their desires and taking actions. If the baseline was low: that person will likely sulk in their suffering and be even more bitter for the rest of their life.

Can you increase your baseline, the baseline coefficient, or is it a given in one person's character? You will not always be able to avoid difficult situations, but you can modify the impact they have on your happiness level by how you choose to respond to the unfavourable external condition. Unhappiness may be caused by regrets, failures and insecurities, by situations we cannot influence, such as heartbreak, loss and fear, bad memories, hatred, angriness, etc. A person could be overly sensitive, overreact to minor things, or take things too personally and take small negative things too seriously and blow them up out of proportion. These are all feelings and emotions, our own interpretation of how an unfavourable external condition can affect us. But all you need to do is analyse the root causes and then decide for each of the causes, either to accept/forgive it (if you can't change it) or to change it. Accept the things you can't change; change the things you can't accept. There are some things, like the weather, that you cannot change. However, there's always something you can do: if you can't stand the cold, move to a warmer climate. If you absolutely can't accept something, then you must take action to change it. The sooner you start accepting the things you cannot change, the more you will increase your baseline coefficient.

A large part of the behaviour, emotions and thought processes are encrypted in the personality and character of a person, which are rather difficult to change. For the part of happiness that stems from conscious behaviour, changes should be possible. When you have awareness, and you feel that improvements are needed, then Chapter 4 provides guidance on how you can increase your baseline level.

The Current External Conditions Equation

Happiness is very subjective, as it depends on the individual and their own perception of the current situation they are in. Happiness has two main drives: the current external (objective) conditions and the current internal (subjective) expectations about those conditions. When the external conditions are higher than the internal expectations, you are likely going to have the feeling of happiness (you have more than you want). On the other hand, when the external conditions are lower than your internal expectations, you are likely going to have the feeling of unhappiness (you have less than you want). When the external conditions are at the same level of your expectations, you will likely feel neutral, a feeling of satisfaction and contentment, but neither elevated feeling of happiness, bliss or joy, nor a troubled feeling of unhappiness (you have what you want).

Happiness does not depend on the external conditions, such as how much money you have, whether you are married or not, how much salary you earn, what sort of car you drive, whether you are obese or not, etc. These external conditions are objective, neutral, and can be easily measured. There is nothing good or bad about the existing conditions; it is your thinking and interpretation of those conditions that makes them good or bad.

Let me give some examples. When you expect a salary raise of 500 and you receive a salary raise of 750, you are likely going to feel happy. On the other hand, when you receive a salary raise of 250, you are likely going to have feelings of unhappiness. When the raise is 500, equalling your expectation, you are likely going to have a feeling of contentment. When you are told that nobody received a salary increase, and that you are the only exception, you are likely going to be happy with 250, even when you were initially expecting 500. That is because you adjusted your expectation from 500 to 0, and the raise of 250 is then still higher than your expectations.
When you are currently driving an old car which frequently breaks down, you are likely going to have a feeling of unhappiness. At the moment that you decide to buy a new car, your internal expectation will rise, and your unhappiness with your old car might increase. When you collect your new car at the dealership, the external conditions are lifted to, or above, the level of your internal expectations, and you are likely going to experience the feeling of happiness (or contentment), because the car will work without interruptions. Usually such feelings of happiness do not last very long, and quickly become neutral again, because the external conditions exactly meet

your internal expectations. You expect your new car to remain shiny and in perfect state for quite a while. When you get a dent two weeks after buying your new car, you will likely experience the feeling of unhappiness. Your internal expectation of the time duration of a perfect car was higher than the actual incurred time for the car being perfect. If you get your first dent after 10 years, you are likely going to have a neutral feeling, because you reasonably expect a 10-year old car to have some dents.

Above examples show that your happiness will depend on how you interpret your situation within the existing external conditions The event itself is neutral, just a fact. Happiness does not come from the outside, it comes from within. According to studies, the external conditions themselves have a weight of about 10% only, whereas the internal expectations about those conditions account for around 90%.

In equation this looks as follows:

The Current External Conditions Equation:
Happiness = Current External Conditions > Current Internal Expectations
Weights: 100% = 10% + 90%

The equation shows that you have two possibilities to increase your happiness level: you can increase the external conditions, so that they become larger than your internal expectations, and/or you can decrease your internal expectations, so that they become lower than the external conditions.

Decreasing your expectations can be done by accepting the situation that you are in, acknowledging that you will not be able to change your specific external condition that brings you unhappiness. When you have a permanent physical handicap, it is unlikely that you will be able to undo that handicap, though, for example, prosthetic limbs have come a far way in enabling physically handicapped people to live a normal life, and even climb the Mount Everest. Jessica Cox (see also Chapter 2) was born without arms, but still managed to reach a state of happiness by building a meaningful and rewarding life. The only way that she could have done that is by lowering her internal expectation of a perfect body, while at the same time setting challenging goals for what she could achieve (driving, piloting, etc.) with the existing conditions of her body. Would she have kept her expectation of a perfect body, she would have been suffering, sulking and feeling unhappy her whole life. Accepting a current external condition for what it is, accepting that you are not able to change it, will often result in a surge of relief, which surge washes away the feelings of unhappiness, returning you to your baseline happiness.

Life will give you ups and downs, ease and struggle, joy and suffering, laughter and tears, happiness and sadness, and relief and pain. It is up to you how you let the negative aspects of life influence the state of our happiness. Will your level of happiness go up and down, synchronised with these influences, or can you temper the negative influences?

There is a way to moderate the influence of suffering. The way is to find a meaning in the suffering, by analysing the reason why this suffering is manifesting in you. Since everything happens for a reason in this Universe, it is up to you to find out what this reason is and what is causing this suffering in the first place. Perhaps you have attracted the suffering through the law of attraction, or perhaps you did not take sufficient actions to prevent suffering, or the actions that you are taking are not effective. Usually the root causes can be reduced to only a few.

For example, for most people a visit to the dentist means suffering when he has to drill close to your nerves, or when teeth are replaced with prosthetics. Setting your internal expectation, that through this suffering your teeth will look nicely again through your radiant smile, will help you accept and undergo the suffering while in the dentist's chair, or the hour in the waiting room preceding your treatment. An example of emotional suffering can be the sadness which occurs when a relationship is ended. There is always a reason and a root cause for ending a relationship. Analyse those reasons and causes, and identify the opportunities that the ended relationship could bring. Look for the positive side. When you come to the conclusion that the relationship was not meant to be, it means that you are now free to find a new relationship that is meant to be. Raise your expectation that being single, and on the search for your perfect partner, fuels your desire and motivation to make the best of the new situation. Positive expectations will often lead to positive results (law of attraction).

Sometimes it is not immediately clear why life is putting you through (emotional or physical) suffering. This is why it is important to keep reflecting on the causes of the suffering, as time passes. It might even take a year or more before it becomes obvious why something happened in your life, at which time you will be able to recognise how much good has come from the period of suffering. Reflecting on suffering with the desire and realisation of a positive expectation will enable you to process your suffering. Finding a meaning to suffering will enable you to accept it, preventing you to become bitter, hung up on the past, angry, disappointed, etc. Look for the meaning in the changes and improve your future life, don't linger in the past.

The fact that the internal expectations are part of the equation automatically means that happiness is subjective. Because it is subjective, it is difficult to objectively measure and determine happiness. Let me now further analyse these internal expectations.

The Current Internal Expectations Equation

Movies, TV, marketing, advertisements and media play an ever increasingly role in shaping society. They shape society by showing ideals to promote their products and services in the form of expensive brand products, luxury life styles and perfectly shaped bodies. These ideals relate to skin, health, physical appearance, family relations, clothing, watches, cars, houses, vacations, hair colour, insurances, banking, and many more, basically all aspects of everybody's life. Ideals sell, because people have an inherent desire for being as good as possible, and through the competitive nature of the humans, being better than other people. Through these mass media, many people can't resist the temptation to lift their expectations to the ideal level that is mirrored in front of them. Men want to have six-pack abdominals shown by many movie actors, they want to drive that 500 horse power car with which successful people are portrayed, women want to have the shape and sizes of the Victoria Secret model, and wear those branded heels that the star wore on the red carpet, teenagers want to have the newest iPhone within two months after its release, etc. Many people who raise their expectations to that level, however, are not able to match those expectations in their external conditions. The result is a gap between these two, leading to the feeling of dissatisfaction with one's current situation and thus unhappiness.

In such cases there are only two ways to restore happiness:

1. You can set the ideal condition (or an inferred condition) as a goal, make an action plan to achieve that goal and consistently and persistently execute that action plan. The following Chapters of this book address this pathway to happiness.

2. You can reduce your wants to your needs, or to such a level that your expectations, at minimum, match your current situation (of the external conditions) again. This is further detailed below, and touched upon in the next Chapters as well.

A need is a condition which is required to fulfil the basic life's requirements for safety, security, health, money to pay for food, protection against the elements (clothing, a walled and roofed home), getting from your home to your work, etc. Needs can be clearly defined, and have a limit, as they generally relate to the minimum external conditions required for survival (in the narrow as well as broad sense of the word).

A want arises when the sought-after expectation exceeds the need. This surplus beyond the need can be called desire. Wants can be limitless, whatever the mind can conceive. As explained before, media play an important role in fuelling the desire element of the expectation, increasing a need to a want.

Wants and needs are not static; they develop as one's life progresses, and differ from person to person. For example, do you want or need a 500 horse power car? If you are an office or factory worker, this is a want. If you are a competitive race driver, this is a need. A 10-room house is a want when you are single, but it is probably a need when you have 15 children. A 200'000 Dollar expensive watch is probably a want for everybody. Eating out at the most expensive restaurants is a need when you are a restaurant tester, but a want when you just love haute cuisine. Travelling around the world is a want when you work in a factory, but a need when you are an author of travel books. Listening to music is a want when you are a teenager in school, but it is a need for the conductor training his orchestra for a performance. As you see, it is possible to transfer a want into a need. Most often that happens when you find your passion and live the purpose of your life. But more of that in Chapter 5.

We can link the wants and needs to the Current Internal Expectations Equation as follows:

The Current Internal Expectations Equation:
Current Internal Expectations (Wants) = Needs + Desires
Weights: 100% = 10% + 90%

More than 75% of the world's population live under the circumstances that their external conditions are at least equal to, or much higher than their needs. When we set the desire element at zero (absence of desires), principally this should mean that the majority of the world's population should be happy. Still, that does not seem to be the case, and you will know many people around you that are unhappy, even though their external conditions are far greater than their needs. This is where the impact of desire becomes visible, and shows how significant this impact is. One can say that for most people in the developed world, the expectations consist in the magnitude of 90% of desire and only 10% of need. How simple would it be to increase the happiness in the world, if we could simply eliminate desires? But this goes against evolution. The human species has progressed throughout the centuries and millions of years, because they were desiring something better, because they were dreaming big. Humans always had, and still have, grand wishes to evolve themselves, their external conditions, their place amongst the other species and their role and contribution in life. It is this desire that has brought us Wi-Fi, cars, the space shuttle, medicines, etc. Are we happier because of these progressive achievements? We should be, as shown above, but are we? From a collective human species perspective desire is good, from a personal perspective desire is good as well, as long as you use it in a positive way, leading you on a path to happiness when it enables you to improve your external conditions. Desire without corresponding improvement actions (progression) will only lead to unhappiness.

At this stage, lets briefly look at the Buddhist perspective on happiness. According to Buddhism, happiness can be obtained by removing all attachments (= desires), because it is this attachment that causes the suffering. One could say that a Buddhist has the desire to be free from desires. When you apply this concept to the Happiness Equation, a Buddhist's formula for happiness is:

Happiness = Current External Conditions > Needs

Since the needs are very basic and mostly relate to the survival of the body, in theory, it should be easy for a Buddhist to reach a state of happiness.

A third element needs to be introduced in the Current Internal Expectations Equation, the element of Belief. In this respect, belief is defined as an internal expectation or anticipation. The use of belief in this

equation is neither meant in the religious sense nor in the sense of the dualistic belief systems about good and bad, right and wrong, etc.
A need and desire alone are insufficient to determine the expectation about an existing external condition. The element of belief is the linking pin, forging the transformation of the needs + desires into the expectations of the current external conditions. Your belief determines why, how, when and how much of your desires you expect to be realised in your external conditions. A strong belief will lead to a high expectation and anticipation of your desire to be realised. A weak belief causes low expectations for the realisation of your desire.

The source of someone's belief can vary. An extremely weak source would be when someone thinks that they simply "deserve" something, without any other source corroborating why this proclaimed entitlement is a valid expectation. Similarly, wishful thinking is a weak source. When belief is based on experience, obtained in successful comparable previous cases, it has a very strong source. Similarly, when belief is based on goal setting and strong actions to achieve those goals, it has a strong basis. In this way, belief based on a weak source may easily lead to over-estimation of the transformation process of the desire into the external conditions, whereas a strong source may lead to a realistic expectation.

When you relate this back to Internal Expectations Equation, you can say that the stronger your belief, the higher the expectation that the desire will be realised, and thus the more certainty (likelihood) is allocated to the realisation of external condition. In this way, strong beliefs may easily lead to disappointments and unhappiness, when the expectations are not met. Having a strong belief is, however, not necessarily bad. It may only create false expectations when you base a strong belief on a weak source. When the belief is based on a strong source, the likelihood of over-estimation will be limited. The lesson to take away for your happiness is therefore to carefully scrutinise the sources of your beliefs that feed your expectations about realisation of your desires. When they are based on weak sources, you can either find stronger sources, or you may have to adjust (lower) your expectations to avoid disappointment and unhappiness.

Earlier you saw that the split between needs and desires is about 10%:90%. When you add beliefs to the equation, the ratios change as follows:

The Current Internal Expectations Equation:

Current Internal Expectations = Needs + Desires + Beliefs
Weights: 100% = 10% + 60% + 30%

The Progression Equation

Hope for a better future is a major contributor to accepting a current situation. Almost all people work towards improving their current situation, and aim for a future situation which reflects their ideals. It is the progression from their current situation towards their goals which is a major influence on the state of happiness of a person. More accurately, happiness from a better future situation is derived from the striving and progression, as well as anticipation, towards that situation.

Improving your current external conditions can be done by setting clear goals and working hard to achieve those goals. For example, if you currently live in a one-bedroom apartment, and you have your second child on the way, you are likely going to feel stressed and unhappy because of insufficient living space for a family of four. You can change these external conditions by setting a clear goal for what you want (a three-bedroom apartment), developing a thoughtful and structured action plan (set a budget, scout the market for lease apartments, plan and schedule your relocation, etc.) to achieve that goal, and then consequently executing your action plan. Although your current existing situation may not be to your satisfaction, knowing that you have a plan and actions to improve that situation will generate feelings of happiness in anticipation of reaching your goal.

In case you would set your goal at a 10-bedroom luxury villa, it is unlikely that will be able to lift your external conditions to that level (when your current external situation is a one-bedroom apartment). In such case, your progression will be limited, and consequently, it won't lead to feelings of happiness.

All of us experience certain events in our progression towards goals, for which it is difficult to understand why they are happening to us. They seem to have no relationship with your goals and your actions, they just seem to pop into your life, coming from nowhere, completely unexpected, completely independent from your thoughts and actions. Sometimes these events are strengthening your flow of life, increasing happiness, sometimes these events go against the flow of your life, and cause hurdles towards your goal achievement, and thus suffering. They are the inexplicable events influencing your progression. For example, you just bought a new car, when it turns out that your wife is pregnant with twins, and the new car will be too small. The value of your real estate increases, because a project developer has announced to build a high-end shopping mall in the vicinity of your house. You arrive at the airport after the departure time of your flight (the last flight of the day), however, at the check-in counter they tell you that the flight was delayed, and they can still check you in.

Your progression towards goals are not only influenced by the goals themselves, and your actions to achieve those goals, but also by an independent factor which can be called Karma. Karma is a term used in Buddhism, and describes the law of cause and effect from a spiritual perspective. When your thoughts and actions are positive, happiness will follow, whereas when your thoughts and actions are negative, suffering will follow. According to Buddhist beliefs, the Karma of your previous life can strongly influence your present life. In other words, positive and negative events might happen to you, for which you can't see a connection in your present life. You could also call this factor Fate or Destiny. The distinction between Fate and Karma is that Karma refers to a belief in a cause and effect triggered by own behaviour, whereas Fate refers to a belief in events, outside your control, that are predetermined by the Universe. For the purpose of this book, I will use Karma to represent uncontrollable, positive and negative, events.

When you divide Progression in its constituent components, the Equation looks as follows:

The Progression Equation:
Progression = Goals + Actions + Karma
Weights: 100% = 10% + 70% + 20%

The external conditions arising from the goals and actions relate to the cause and effect generated by yourself, whereas the Karma element relates to the cause and effect of events which are generated outside your observable influence. This way of analysing happiness is pushing into unknown territory and, to my knowledge, no research data is available allocating weights to each of these components. From my personal experience, as someone with clear goals and structured actions, however, the above weights seem to make sense. Look at it as follows. When a person sets no goals for the progression of their life, and takes no actions to steer their life, everything that happens to that person will seem like karma. That person will feel that they live in an uncontrollable environment where (positive and negative) events just happen to them. This makes sense, because when you set the weights for goals and actions at 0%, the karma weight automatically becomes 100%. On the other hand, when you set clear goals and take all necessary actions to reach those goals, you will feel that you control and steer the progression and direction of your life, although certain unanticipated and uncontrollable events will still enter your life. But you won't feel overwhelmed by these events, that seem to come out of nowhere. The stronger your goals and your actions to achieve these goals, the weaker the influence of karma on your progress and happiness derived from your progress.

The next Chapters are all about goals and actions, and will assist you in better managing these two components.

The Happiness Cycle

The elements of the Happiness Equation can be tied together forming the Happiness Cycle. From a process point of view, the starting point of happiness often lies in the initiation (or reduction or removal) of a desire. This then causes a chain reaction. Your desire for a certain external condition will move you to set a goal. The desire also fuels the continuous stream of actions, till the goal is reached. As a general rule, you can say that the higher a desire, the stronger the actions. The stronger your goal and actions, the lower the influence of karma will be on your happiness level. The progression itself will give you feelings of happiness, as will the anticipation of reaching your goal. In this sense, the goal is a desired future state of the external condition, with the intention that this future external condition equals or exceeds the internal expectation for that situation. Your existing, current external condition flows through your happiness baseline, where it is judged. This judgement is then passed on to your internal expectations, resulting in a feeling of unhappiness, contentment or happiness. In case of unhappy feelings, the desire will be increased, and the cycle starts again.

In effect this means that your happiness is mostly influenced by your desires, by pursuing those desires through clear goals and focussed actions.

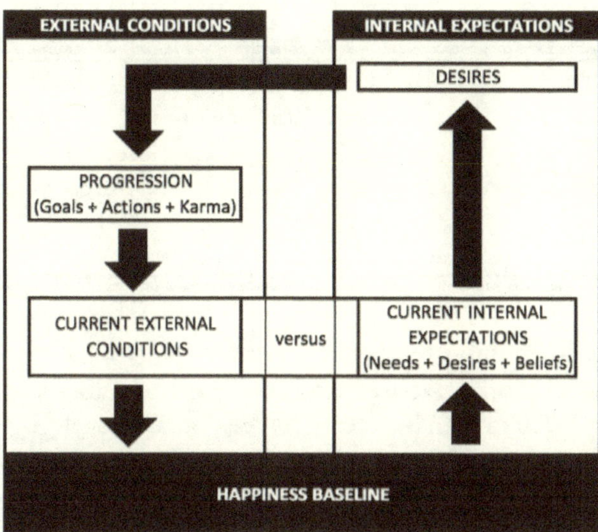

This Happiness Cycle is captured in the Universal Happiness Formula in the next section.

The Universal Happiness Formula

So far the following Happiness Equations are developed:

Happiness = Fixed Baseline Coefficient + Variable Other Factors Weights: 100% = 40% + 60%

Happiness = Current External Conditions > Current Internal Expectations Weights: 100% = 10% + 90%

Current Internal Expectations = Needs + Desires + Beliefs Weights: 100% = 10% + 60% + 30%

Progression = Goals + Actions + Karma Weights: 100% = 10% + 70% + 20%

When we integrate these equations, the following Universal Happiness Formula emerges:

Happiness =
Baseline Coefficient
+
(Current External Conditions > (Needs + Desires + Beliefs))
+
(Goals + Actions + Karma)

From a controlling point of view there are several levels.

- Goals, Actions, Desires and Beliefs are fully under your own control. That means you can set them at any level (high or low) that you think is right for your life.
- The Baseline Coefficient is mostly predetermined by your genes, as they have been passed on by your ancestors. Still, there are possibilities to elevate your baseline level, in case you have the self-awareness that this might be too low. The baseline has to do with the way you think, and since thinking is fully under your own control, the level of the baseline is under your control. The critical aspect for improvement is the self-awareness, which will lead to control. Chapter 4 elaborates on methods to lift your happiness baseline.
- The Current External Conditions result from your past goals, past actions and past karma. Since all causes lie in the past, you can't change them anymore, and it is like it is. The only way you can change your current external conditions is through progression with present/future actions towards your goals.
- Needs have been predetermined by nature and evolution. Though you may be able to slightly change your basic needs, generally the survival of your organism requires a minimum level of care.
- Karma represent events, impacting your external conditions, over which you have no direct control.

When you add the percentages to the levels of impact, the following emerges:

Happiness =
Baseline Coefficient (BC) + (Current External Conditions (CEC) > (Needs + Desires + Beliefs)) + (Goals + Actions + Karma)

BC +	(CEC >	(Needs +	Desires +	Beliefs)) +	(Goals +	Actions +	Karma)
40%+ (			20%	) + (		40%	)
40%+ (	10%	(	90%	)) + (		40%	)
40%+ (	10%	(10%	60%	30%)) + (	10%	70%	20%)
40%+ (	**2% +**	**(2% +**	**11% +**	**5%)) + (**	**4% +**	**28% +**	**8%)**

The Baseline Coefficient counts for 40% of your happiness level. Through self-awareness and mind training, you are able to positively influence your baseline.

Your Current External Conditions versus your Current Internal Expectations contribute only 20% to your happiness level. Your Internal Expectations, consisting of Needs, Desires and Beliefs, have an influence of 18% (2% + 11% + 5%), making a large part under your own control.

Happiness derived from Progression and anticipation towards your goals for an improved future external condition counts for 40% of your total happiness, of which 32% (4% + 28%) is under your own control.

Added together, you have direct control over 90% (40% + 18% + 32%) of the elements that influence your state of happiness.

From the non-controllable 10%, 8% relates to Karma and 2% relates to the Current External Conditions (when we consider the latter as an as-is incurred state).

Due to the inherent difficulty of measuring happiness, these percentages are neither based on an exact science, nor is full empirical evidence available to support this precise calculation of the weights in the Happiness Equation. Additionally, some of the percentages may need to be personalised, in case your individual values deviate from the above standard. Still, the above equation and their weights are extremely useful in identifying the main levers for happiness. The purpose of the Universal Happiness Formula is to make happiness and the quest for happiness transparent, understandable, measurable and manageable.

If anyone states that their happiness is out of their control, that life is just throwing unhappiness at them, that they can't find a pathway out of unhappy circumstances, that their happiness is dependent on other people, then they are clearly not aware of the Universal Happiness Formula. Because the opposite is true. You control your own happiness. Happiness is derived from elements which are under your own control for around 90%. Approximately half of these elements are relatively easily influenced, by changing your way of thinking through a structured and methodical approach, and by setting clear goals and by progressing towards your goals through consistent actions. The other half, relating to your baseline coefficient, is much more difficult to influence as it relates to behaviour captured in your genes. It means changing yourself and how you perceive the world around you.

Since 90% is under your own control, this also means that correctly and consistently applying this Universal Happiness Formula will almost certain lead to enduring happiness.

The Happiness Portfolio (further developed in the remaining Chapters), follows the principles of the Universal Happiness Formula and applies these to your everyday life. Four main sources influence your level of happiness on a practical day-to-day basis: the state of your health, the state of your material wealth, the state of your mind and your spiritual state. Continue to read the next chapters and start your journey through the Happiness Portfolio, to explore and aim for an all-around happiness in all aspects of your life. When followed, the Formula in combination with the Portfolio, have the intense power to achieve happiness for everybody, everywhere, anytime. As with achieving any goal in your life, of course, this needs clarity, courage, determination, and persistence. But when you follow through, happiness will surely come to you, with the (90%) certainty of the outcome of a mathematical formula.

Chapter 2

HAPPINESS FROM YOUR PHYSICAL STATE

Introduction

Biological and physiological needs are the lowest level, the basics of all the other needs, which need to be fulfilled first, in order for the fragile human body to survive. From an evolutionary perspective, this is where your forefathers developed their first feelings of happiness. They were happy when they found a dry cave, when their hunt for food was successful, when they could warm by a fire, when they were close to a crystal clear river and when the animal furs kept them warm during the cold days. Their happiness level was motivated by their level of physical well-being in their everyday struggle for survival in a brutal natural environment.

These basics are generally taken for granted in the modern developed world, as far as they relate to clean water, sufficient food, clean air, warm shelter, protective clothing, and adequate sleep. You have a roofed place to sleep and shelter you from the weather, you only need to walk or drive to a nearby supermarket to obtain your food, drinkable water comes out of the tap, you have clothing to protect you against the cold, etc. The thing with these basic needs is, when you have them, you take them for granted. And taking them for granted means that you don't attach a feeling of happiness to them.

For people living in a developing country, the fulfilment of these basic needs may not be guaranteed. Several parts of the world regularly experience severe draughts for extended periods of time, causing shortage of drinking water. People living under such conditions may have to walk many hours to get their day ration for washing, drinking and cooking. They don't take this basic need for granted, and if they would be transferred to the basic luxuries of the developed world, surely their happiness level would spike, until they have gotten used to this and take it for granted as well.

Your physical state can be split into three main elements: the state of your body, the state of your health and your vitality (energy) level. Your level of happiness with your physical state will be derived from setting clear objectives for each of these three elements, assessing your current status, and taking actions to close the gap to your desired state.

Perfect Body

For the happiness derived from your bodily state, you will need to set a goal and define what a perfect body means to you. Perfection is in the eye of the beholder, so only you can define that for yourself. For example, a person with only one leg might define perfect as getting a prosthetic leg, so that they can walk and run again, and even climb the Mount Everest. For a person that is obese, a perfect body could be to have only 30% body fat, whereas a professional bodybuilder may define perfect at only 5% body fat. For a woman it could mean enlarging her breasts, or making her breasts smaller, changing the hair colour to blond or red, getting rid of cellulite, etc. For a man it could mean having the body features of Ryan Reynolds (six pack and all), or growing that beard. There are certain physical traits which you won't be able to change, such as your height, bone structure, etc., but most of your body features are changeable. Your appearance, including weight, is usually the most recognisable feature of your bodily state.
The way it works with goals, is that they have to be specific, detailed, concrete, measurable and with a deadline, so sufficiently detail your bodily goals. Set your goals as an ideal vision for yourself, set it to a value that means "perfect" to you. What does your perfect body look like?
Next you measure where you currently stand against the values that you defined as goal, resulting in a gap analysis. Seeing a gap might not make you happy; it could even depress you, depending on the size of the gap. But

don't worry. The whole point is that your happiness level will surely increase commensurately your progress to your goal of a perfect body.
List the activities that are needed to close the gap. It might mean doing more physical workouts, such as fitness, cardio, yoga, walking, swimming, cycling, hiking, dancing, running or playing in team sports, in order to increase the burning of calories. It might mean reducing the intake of calories, by having a healthy diet of low carbs and high protein food. The fitness of your body is strongly influenced by alcohol, nicotine, caffeine and other substances. Assess whether you need to reduce or completely eliminate these. Your skin looks pale from being too much indoors? The appearance of a healthy body is supported by a tanned skin colour. Enjoy the sunshine, while wearing adequate UV-protection.

Perfect Health

The thing with health is, when you have it, you take it for granted. Only when you lose your health, either temporarily or permanently, through accident or disease, do you realise how important this is. As a consequence, when you always have good health, generally it won't lead to a conscious feeling of happiness. That feeling of happiness for being healthy often returns when you are recovering from a physical weakness caused by illness or injury. You probably felt very miserable, and thus unhappy, when you were seriously ill or got into that accident, causing limitations to your daily routines. But how long did your feeling of happiness last, once you were back in your old routines? I bet not very long.

Normally you expect your body to operate within the boundaries of the Standard Operating Procedures (SOPs) for the human body. These SOPs relate to the motions of your limbs (so that you can move), the functioning of your lungs (so that you can breathe), the effectiveness of your five senses (so that you can interpret your outside world), the clarity of your thinking processes (so that you can give direction to your life), the functioning of your organs (so that your body continues to work), etc. Still, how many things do you do to your body that are against these SOPs? Many people smoke, drink too high quantities of alcohol, or use drugs, eat too much, consume too high quantities of fat, sweets or unnaturally sugared food (as in soft drinks), and get insufficient vitamins from their deep-fried food. Some people have dark rings around their eyes and look unhealthy pale from too much stress, too long working hours, too little sleep, too little fresh air and sunshine, and too little exercise. Some people accumulate fat around their waist, and carry around big bellies. Many people eat more than their energy output requires, and eat at the wrong times for their energy requirement, such as shortly before going to sleep. People with such habits often look 10 years older than they are, and will often have a life expectancy that is 10 years lower than the average. You probably know quite a few people to whom some or all of these descriptions apply.

What motivates these people to act against the SOPs for their body? There are probably two main reasons. First, the short term, temporary, pleasures derived from such unhealthy behaviour outshine the awareness for the long term, permanent, damage. What is immediately in front of you (in time and/or distance), usually receives much more attention than what is still miles or years away. Second, the behaviour pattern is often influenced by circumstances over which the person believes he/she has no control. The typical examples are a demanding job, long working hours, old settled habits and social pressures. These reasons are, however, relatively easy to counter by raising the awareness level for the long forgotten happiness derived from health, by setting long term goals for the physical state of the body and changing the behaviour to achieve these long term goals. It might take a long time and endurance to achieve these goals, but it can be done.

Your body is the carrying vehicle of your soul. Your mind, at the conscious and subconscious levels, controls and commands your body. So change your mind's perspective on your body, and you can achieve a perfect physical health. Set your mind to take care of, and love the carrying vehicle, your body, for without it, you will cease to exist. You have only one body; there is no spare in the garage, you can't go and buy a new one. Love and maintain your body as you love and maintain your car, which you shine and polish, have regularly checked and greased, ensuring it has enough oil and gasoline (without overflowing).

For your happiness from perfect health, you will need to set a goal and define what perfect health means to you. Never to be ill? To recover from your present illness? Set your goals as an ideal vision for yourself; set it to a value that means "perfect" to you. Next you measure where you currently stand (your status quo) against the values that you defined as goal, and list the activities that are needed to close the gap. It might mean getting more sleep. So you might have to go to bed earlier. It might mean getting better quality of sleep. So you might have to stop watching TV/news shortly before going to bed, as negativity will stay on your mind when it is the last thing your brain records before it shuts down. In this respect, try to "program" your subconscious mind in a positive way before going to sleep. Don't eat two hours before you go to sleep, as otherwise the activities of your digestive organs will prevent a deep sleep. It might mean changing to a healthy diet of low carbs and high protein food, vegetables, fruits and balanced vitamins. Your health is strongly influenced by alcohol, nicotine, caffeine and other substances, which weaken your immune system. Assess whether you need to reduce or completely eliminate these.

High Vitality

For your happiness from high vitality, you will need to set a goal and define what high vitality means to you. Do you want to feel and look young and maintain high levels of energy, even when you get into the progressive years of age? Set your goals as an ideal vision for yourself, set it to a value that means "perfect" to you. Next you measure where you currently stand against the values that you defined as goal, and list the activities that are needed to close the gap. It might mean getting more and undisturbed sleep. It might mean staying physically active, also after your retirement. It might mean that you will need to keep developing your mind with new knowledge and that you keep learning and keep developing your spiritual wisdom by reading relevant books.

Compared to the three other "States", as described in the following three Chapters, the goals for the Physical State are generally the easiest to achieve. Sure, it means hard work to become and remain fit and healthy, but it is fully within your own control. That means that the level of happiness derived from your physical state solely depends on the level of efforts that you need and want to put in. There are many examples of perfect bodies, for women as well as for men, in the media, in movies and on the runways for the high-fashion brands. In case you set a tough physical goal for yourself, have them serve as an example. Health is very much considered a private and personal matter, which is not often shared with the world. Do you know someone with perfect health, who has never been ill and lives vibrantly till an old age? Use that person as an example when you are pondering what you need to do to achieve that as well. The Earth's population is getting older as people live longer due to advancements in medicine, hygiene and general living and care conditions. You must know actors that work till in their seventies or even eighties, and still look vibrant and full of energy. Strive for vitality, even when getting older, and you will continue to experience happiness.

Examples of Special Achievement

Some examples of special achievements from the Physical State:

- Arnold Schwarzenegger: he became bodybuilding champion from when he was 20, and continued to expand his career based on his physical traits through acting in movies for many years. Through these activities he provided entertainment for many millions of people.
- Gisele Bündchen: she is a so called "supermodel", and was one of Victoria's Secret Angels. She is a Goodwill Ambassador for the United Nations Environment Programme, has acted in several movies and supports many charities.
- Jessica Cox: she was born without arms, and received the US Inspiration Award for Women in 2012. She is the world's first armless pilot, and holds a black-belt in Taekwondo as the first armless person.

The last example shows that a serious inhibition does not have to exclude happiness. Jessica must have adjusted/personalised the goals for her Physical State, in order to still make them challenging and attainable. She has probably already achieved more goals for her Physical State than any of us will ever achieve.

These are of course extreme examples of people reaching this high level of achievement. Let them serve as a source of inspiration, while you ponder about your own goals and actions for achieving happiness for your Physical State.

Applying the Universal Happiness Formula

Happiness = Baseline Coefficient + (Current External Conditions > (Needs + Desires + Beliefs)) + (Goals + Actions + Karma)

The first element generating happiness from your Physical State is the level of your Baseline Coefficient. A high baseline would mean that you accept your body for what it is at present and the way it looks naturally. A low baseline would mean that you are self-critical about each and every little flaw of your body. You will be much happier when you simply accept the pure reality that you need to work with, before you start the fine-tuning towards your goals.

Your Needs relate to the fact that you need to eat, drink, sleep, maintain your body temperature, whatever the weather conditions, etc.

The next element of happiness will be generated by your Desires, which fuel Goal setting and Actions to achieving those Goals. Determine your desire for your body, health and vitality, and from there derive your goals and actions. In case your desire is significantly higher than your present status, you will have a gap to close. Be realistic about the time needed to close this gap, and set your goal at an achievable, but challenging, level to avoid frustration.

The above elements are all under your own control. Karma may play a role when you fall ill or get an injury, which may temporarily stop or reverse the progress that you have made towards your goals. Keep believing in the goals and pick up the pace again once you have recovered.

There is a direct link between physical exercise, health and the feeling of well-being. Physical exercise generates feelings of happiness because it stimulates the production of Serotonin and Endorphins in your Brain, which make you feel better, improve your mood, give more self-confidence, etc. It can generate feelings of success (for having achieved an exercise goal) and it improves the functioning of the brain. Physical exercise helps the bodily circulation and strengthens the immune system.

Your Physical State deserves attention and priority, as without it, you will cease to exist. Don't take it for granted, but treasure it and keep maintaining your body, health and vitality, and you will find enduring happiness from these three elements.

Your Physical State Happiness Portfolio

The Happiness Portfolio for your Physical State contains three main elements: your bodily state, your health state and the state of your vitality.

Work on these three elements, accept what you have to work with, and you will be able to derive happiness from your Physical State as follows:

happiness from	Example Goals	Present status	Example activities to achieve goals
YOUR PHYSICAL STATE			
PERFECT BODY	Slim and fit body, xxkg and xx% fat by dd/mm/yy	to be filled out by YOU	-regular physical workouts, like yoga, fitness, walking -healthy diet: low carbs, high protein -no alcohol, no smoking or other substances -regular sun tanning (with protection)
PERFECT HEALTH	Perfect health, free from illnesses by dd/mm/yy	to be filled out by YOU	-enough and deep sleep: don't watch tv/news shortly before going to sleep, program your subconscious mind in a positive way before going to sleep -no eating two hours before sleep -healthy food & drinks: vegetables and fruit; balanced vitamins
HIGH VITALITY	Vital, young looking and feeling by dd/mm/yy	to be filled out by YOU	-sufficient and deep undisturbed sleep -be physically active -keep learning and develop the mind with knowledge. Increase your spiritual wisdom by reading relevant books.

Chapter 3

HAPPINESS FROM YOUR MATERIAL STATE

Introduction

The next level is your material state, which, to a certain extent, relates to the needs for safety and security. This relates to your material environment, your physical safety, financial security, emotional security, order, law and societal stability. These can probably roughly be split in two categories: materialism and society, where the society plays the role of protecting your materialism.

Most countries in the world have adequate societal and juridical systems in place to protect the citizen's materiality. In those countries, order, law, security, safety and stability are more or less a given, making this an important contributor to the level of happiness. Because the benefits from living in an ordered and regulated society are a given for most of the world's population, this topic is not further addressed in the Happiness Portfolio. Should you be living in a country or area where societal order is not a given, then it should become an element of your Happiness Portfolio, with its own Goals and Actions.

Wants and Needs

You should not confuse your Wants with your Needs. This is particularly valid for your Material State. Wants, at the materiality level, are one of the most common causes of unhappiness, particularly when wants are derived from the comparison of your own material state with the material state of another person. In such a case your wants are likely causing a large gap to your needs. In itself there is nothing wrong with having material wants, as long as those wants do not lead to unhappiness. Once you have obtained a certain want (for example a nice car), it won't last long before that happiness feeling disappears while you get used to having that nice car. Then is it common that the want is refreshed for having a second car or a more luxurious model of the car, and so an unhappiness feeling might crop up again, as you establish that you don't have what you want. Deriving happiness from your material state is very tricky, as we as humans have the tendency to believe that the material state is never enough, and can always be better.

What is the solution to this problem inherent in the nature of mankind? There are several approaches that might work for you:

- reduced your Wants, to center around your Needs. If there is a big gap to be bridged, you will feel liberated, once you realise that all you need in your material life is provided by your needs.
- Better control your mind, the way you look at your Material State, in order to generate happiness from your material state. If your mind is in a state of deep inner peace and tranquillity, you won't be disturbed anymore by your material wants. Please read the next Chapter about happiness from you Mind State for more details.
- Develop your Spiritual State, in particular your Self-Actualisation. When you find the purpose of your life, and live it with all the passion you have, you are likely automatically improving the life of other people. In such a case your main goal has to be to improve the life of other people (and derive happiness from that), which has a side-effect that your material state significantly improves at the same time (as a secondary goal). When your material state is only a secondary goal in the hierarchy of all goals, you overcome the tendency to believe that the level of your material state is never enough, as you attach less importance to it. This topic is further explored in Chapter 5.

You may even argue that it is possible to completely eliminate the material state from the Happiness Portfolio. Buddhism teaches that everything is impermanent, so that there is no value in attaching one's emotions to the attainment of material objects. Having deep inner peace and tranquillity without attachments to a material state, might lead to higher happiness.

Financial Independence

Financial Independence means having all the money you need to do what you need to do. In such a case financial independence will lead to ultimate happiness. Note that I am not saying what you "want" to do. I intentionally express it as "need", because of the need for Self-Actualisation and Self-Transcendence. Reaching these latter two spiritual levels, and then staying at these spiritual levels, will result in happiness in an enduring way. You will read more about that in Chapter 5.

What you do with your financial independence is essential to the level and duration of your happiness from this material state. Financial independence should never be the ultimate goal; it should be a means to an end. Let me elaborate.

Those people who solely seek materiality and financial independence for the purpose of amassing material things for the pure enjoyment of those material things themselves, will never find lasting happiness. What they want will be significantly more than what they need, for the wants the sky is the limit, meaning that satisfaction will never be achieved. Let me give an example. Toilets come in many forms, shapes, designs and materials. All toilets serve the same purpose, and fulfil the same needs. Still, some people want to have a toilet made out of gold. Why? Not because it serves a different purpose; the functioning of the toilet will be the same as a normal porcelain toilet. They want to have one made out of gold, because they can afford to buy one and want to rise above competition with others, show that they are "better" than others. Wanting to have something in order to be better in comparison with other people, will never lead to lasting happiness, because such happiness is based on an illusion. It is the illusion that happiness can be derived from comparison to others, whereas happiness can only be lasting when it is generated by an inward expectation. When you compare yourself to other people that look rich, you may be falling in a trap. Looking rich does not equal being rich. It might actually be

the bank that owns much of the shown richness, instead of the person that shows off with the material items.
Wanting, but not being able to afford, is an extremely strong force creating unhappiness. The only way to counter this force, and use it to generate happiness, is to reduce your wants to your needs.

A distinctive difference, between the Materiality State and the three other States in the Happiness Portfolio, is that materiality will only lead to happiness when it is put to use for the other three elements of your Happiness Portfolio. Thus having amassed a fortune, and spending a part of that fortune on charity, good causes and improving the life of other people, will generate lasting happiness from that fortune. Having a fortune and behaving like Scrooge McDuck, who swims in a warehouse full of coins for his personal enjoyment of his fortune, will not lead to happiness. As happened to Scrooge McDuck, the sole focus and overly attachment to fortune will lead to fears about losing the fortune. These fears will lead to unhappiness, as the mind will look for ways to desperately maintain the attachment to the fortune, while outside influences will create energy into putting the fortune to good use.

Should you then refrain from setting a goal for your Material State, your Financial Independence? No, you should not. Having a challenging goal for financial independence is a worthy way of enabling happiness for the other three States within your Happiness Portfolio, in particular when it is put to use for the improvement of the life of other people (see Chapter 5). Examples of actions to achieve financial independence are as follows:

- Have a structured and thoughtful plan to get from where you are today to your financial independence. Put in sufficient planning efforts and carefully think through your decisions before putting them into action. Support your approach with risk assessments and risk management. Of course you will need to define what financial independence means to you and put a concrete number and deadline in your goals.
- Develop multiple sources of income. It is rare that independence is generated by only one source of income. You need to diversify in order to increase the odds of generating financial income streams that lead to independence.
- Steer your spending. Focus your spending on those aspects which help you progress in your Happiness Portfolio. As explained

before, being Scrooge McDuck will not lead to happiness from financial independence.

- Link the purpose of your financial independence to the other elements of the Happiness Portfolio, particularly to the goal of improving the life of other people. But don't wait with improving the life of other people till you have achieved financial independence. Progress on both elements goes hand in hand, and your efforts and actions to improve the life of other people might actually spawn your financial independence. Money needs to flow, and spending money on charity, for example, will bring more money to you (law of attraction, cause and effect).

Aim to get financially independent slowly, not quickly. Other than through means that are against the other elements of the Happiness Portfolio, financial independence will come slowly. So have patience and endurance and never give up. If you expect to become financially independent quickly, you will be unhappy, because that expectation is unlikely to come true.

Time Independence

A second important aspect of the Material State is "time". Time is money. Expressed in different words: time is as precious as money and enables goals to be achieved. Look at earning interest on a sum of money at the bank. The passing of time generates money based on certain economic principles. When you look at this from a more spiritual perspective, it seems that time and money are interchangeable. That is why you can cluster time together with money in the Material State.

Time Independence means that you have all the time you need to achieve what you need to achieve. You will reach the highest level of happiness when you have all the time to do what you need to do. Note that I am not saying what you "want" to do. I intentionally express it as "need", because of the need for Self-Actualisation and Self-Transcendence, similar to the explanation about the Financial Independence. Having the time to reach these levels and then stay at these spiritual levels will result in happiness in an enduring way. You will read more about that in Chapter 5.

To relate this topic in an example to myself: the passion in and purpose of my life is to write non-fiction books, which help other people advance in their life. In order to realise my Self-Actualisation, I need time to sit down and develop these books in the creative process of writing. When I was still bound in a corporate job, I did not have the time to realise this Self-Actualisation. Only after I removed the time-shackles from the corporate job, could I allocate sufficient time to find and live my passion. My Time Independence gave me all the time to do what I needed to do. Although I now spend many hours researching, thinking and writing for my books, I still have the feeling of time independence, providing me with the highest level of happiness in this aspect of my Material State.

What does your time independence look like? What does it mean for you? Time independence does not relate to having nothing to do. That would become very boring very quickly, and would lead to feelings of unhappiness because there is no progress with achievement to a certain goal attached to it. In essence, time independence means having sufficient time available to work on, and progress with, the other elements of your Happiness Portfolio. Only in that case will time independence lead to enduring happiness. The following actions can be considered:

- Develop a clear view what you want to achieve with Time Independence. Why do you want to achieve this and how will you want to spend your time once you have it available?
- Contrary to Financial Independence, Time Independence can be achieved easily and quickly in the short term, as it is fully under your own control. In principle you could leave your current job and have all the time available for what you need to do. Many people have done this and achieve an enduring happiness because they reallocated their time to live the purpose of their life.
- Assess the impact of your actions on the other elements of your Happiness Portfolio. Through the reallocation of time, you can change your source of income, and unless you already have Financial Independence, the new source of income should of course be sufficient to cover the basic needs (food, shelter, safety, health, etc.). In this respect, time independence should not lead to significant shortfalls in the level of happiness derived from the other elements of your Happiness Portfolio.

It is noteworthy that you might be able to achieve Financial Independence, without achieving Time Independence. Such would be the case when you are progressing with your career, this career provides you adequate financial awards, however, your passion lies somewhere else, and you don't consider your present career the purpose of your life. Very often, people put so

much efforts in attaining financial independence (through long hours invested in a career), that all other elements of the Happiness Portfolio significantly suffer and fall short on any goal achievement (most likely because no such goals for the other States of the Happiness Portfolio have been set). In such case a person might have all the money they want, but they do not do what they need to do, nor do they have the time to do what they need to do (i.e. following their passion), as all their time is locked-in.
The other way around is of course also possible. A person may have time independence, living the purpose of their life, but that does not necessarily lead to financial independence. It will need the focussed actions described for financial independence to reach that level.

Examples of Special Achievement

Clearly recognisable examples of people who have reached a high level of Financial and Time Independence:

- Donald Trump: he made his name and fame in the footsteps of his father, as a real estate developer. He gathered significant wealth through many more business ventures, supported by his celebrity status. Though often a controversial person, he seems to have Time Independence, as he is in the running for President of the United States during 2015/2016.
- Mark Zuckerberg: he is the living example of how chasing your passion, making all the time available to do what he needs to do to bring his Facebook venture to life, resulted in significant wealth and time to do what he needs to do. In 2015 he announced to transfer 99% of his Facebook stock to a charitable-based venture for the benefit of children of future generations.
- JK Rowling: she followed her passion by taking time to write the Harry Potter book series (even when her books were rejected by many publishers at first), which made her financially independent, having sold more than 450 million copies worldwide.

These are of course extreme examples of people achieving this high level of materiality. Let them serve as a source of inspiration, while you ponder about your own Goals and Actions for achieving happiness from your Material State.

Applying the Universal Happiness Formula

Happiness = Baseline Coefficient + (Current External Conditions > (Needs + Desires + Beliefs)) + (Goals + Actions + Karma)

The first element generating happiness from your Material State is the level of your Baseline Coefficient. A high baseline would mean that you accept your current financial circumstances and time availability for what it is and what you can do with them. A low baseline would mean that you are always comparing yourself with other people and you always feel that you are done short. You will be much happier when you simply realise and acknowledge that you already have all the material items and time you need to live a safe and secure life.

The next element of happiness will be generated by your Desires, which fuel Goal setting and Actions to achieving those Goals. Determine your desire for your Financial and Time Independence, and from there derive your goals and actions. In case your desire is significantly higher than your present status, you will have to close a gap. Be realistic how much time it needs to close this gap, and set your goal at a realistic, but challenging, level to avoid frustration. Financial independence gaps usually take a longer time to close, whereas time independence gaps could be closed quickly.

The difficulty with the Financial Independence element of your Material State is that it largely depends on others (external sources). Sure, it is you who will need to set a goal and initiate actions, but the money can only come to you from the outside. This is in stark contradiction to your Physical State. This means that the Karma element plays a more important role in the formula for happiness of your Material State. Fortunately, there are many ways that you can reduce the role of Karma. You can use the law of attraction, the way you think about money, etc. Expand your mind by reading books on these topics; the Bibliography at the end of this book provides you with a list of recommended reading.

As Buddhism shows, you don't necessarily need your Material State (or at least the Desire element in the formula) to lead an overall meaningful and happy life. So make sure that you give your Material State a level of focus and attention which is balanced within your overall Happiness Portfolio.

Your Material State Happiness Portfolio

You will have noticed that this element of your Happiness Portfolio does not include any pertinent statements about material items, such as a house, a car, brand clothing or expensive accessories such as watches and handbags, etc. The reason is that these are derived from the Financial Independence, where the Financial Independence is the higher cause for generating happiness, not the acquisition of a car or house. Having the material goal of driving a Ferrari or owning a yacht is rather a possible consequence from achieving the financial independence goal. These purely material goals may work well for generating happiness from the process of goal achievement, but they will not work for generating enduring happiness from the goal itself. Happiness from the newest luxury toy is usually short-lived, at maximum until a new toy enters the top of the want list. This is one of the marketing strategies where Apple is really good at, and manages to earn billions of Dollars from the material wants (as opposed to the needs of people who use a phone), when many millions of people renew their Want each time a new model of the iPhone comes out.

The happiness portfolio for your material state looks as follows:

happiness from	Example Goals	Present status	Example activities to achieve goals
YOUR MATERIAL STATE			
FINANCIAL INDEPENDENCE	Have all the money you need to do what you need to do by dd/mm/yy	to be filled out by YOU	-structured and thoughtful long term planning followed by consistent and persistent actions -develop multiple sources of income -control your spending, by spending for the right causes, and be patient -link your financial independence goal to the other elements of the Happiness Portfolio
TIME INDEPENDENCE	Have all the time you need to do what you need to do by dd/mm/yy	to be filled out by YOU	-develop a clear view what you want to achieve with time independence -follow thoughtful and structured actions to realise independence, though these actions can be easily and quickly done -assess the impact of these actions on the other elements of the Portfolio

Chapter 4

HAPPINESS FROM YOUR MIND STATE

Introduction

In Chapter 1 you already read about the concept of happiness. Happiness emerges in your mind, making your mind the real source for the feelings of joy, satisfaction, contentment and fulfilment. The more you can manage and control this source, the happier and at peace with yourself and the world around you, you will become. The mind can be influenced and directed towards happiness when you are sufficiently aware of this and practise certain habits. For this reason, happiness from your Mind State is a part of its own within your Happiness Portfolio.

Deep Inner Peace and Tranquillity

When your mind is in a state of deep inner peace and tranquillity, no outward influence can affect your level of happiness. In order to arrive at this level, you need an inner discipline bringing about a transformation of your attitudes, outlook and perspective on life and the world around you. The greater the state of calmness of your mind, the more you will be able to achieve happiness and joy in your life. Deep inner peace and tranquillity can be generated by three main elements: by controlling your mind, by living in the moment and by leading a simple life.

Control Your Mind

Controlling your mind, keeping a steady peace of mind, despite the always changing circumstances around you, is not easy to accomplish. Your mind records every event, no matter how small, and interprets every event in its own way. Much too often, we let a small, insignificant event completely take over our mood, as the mind blows up a negligible circumstance into something of enormous proportions. How often does it happen that you get upset because your hotel room looks out on a wall instead of on the beach, the soup you get served is cold, you have a small dent in your new car, the music of your kids is too loud, your French manicured nail breaks off, a co-worker criticises you for trying too hard, you are in a traffic jam and late for an appointment, the store does not have your shoe size, your flight is cancelled, you hurt your toe on a toy your kids did not put away, your child spills juice over herself, your neighbour's lawnmower makes a loud noise, it is raining on your day off, your mother-in-law criticises you for how you raise your children, etc. I am sure that you can think of many more examples from your own life. Some of these topics may upset you, some perhaps don't. Some of these topics may make your mind run out of control, start causing worries, may result in sleepless nights and put a severe strain on your relationships. But did your worrying reduce or eliminate your suffering? No it did not, rather the opposite is true; it increased your suffering. Instead of accepting something the way it is, as it can't be undone anymore, instead of forgiving the person who did not intentionally want to upset you, your mind only went deeper into the topic and increased your level of suffering. But this is not necessary; this (and all) suffering can all be avoided by controlling your state of mind.

Don't you usually concentrate your mind on topics that you are unhappy with? Evaluate yourself: how much time in a day you do spend thinking about topics which have resulted in happiness, and as such are generating happy thoughts in your consciousness? Conversely, how much time in a day do you spend thinking about topics, which could potentially disturb or ruin your happiness? Aren't you usually thinking more about the things that you don't want? Don't you occupy most of your mind with risks, what would happen if a negative scenario occurs? And how often do these negative scenarios occur? Do you think about what would happen if a positive scenario occurs? Usually a lot less, I bet. If you listen to conversations of others, how often are people complaining versus expressing their contentment with their life? It seems that there is an extreme focus on the negative, discontentment, and unhappiness in our daily expressions and communications. How often does a boss compliment a staff member, versus how often does a boss criticise a staff member? Isn't this unfair and out of balance, leaning to the negative? Training your mind, to focus on only the good and positive things in your life and in the world, is possible. It is possible to significantly shift your thought processes from a negative inclination to the positive side. And how much relief from worrying, and additional happiness, will that bring!

As long as you lead an active life, participating in the world around you, you are bound to encounter events which have a negative influence on your mind, causing a bad mood. From the larger perspective, many of these events will relate to small, trivial topics and are of a very temporary nature. In reality, an event is just an event; it is a neutral occurrence taking place and affecting your life. It is really your mind which decides how to interpret this occurrence. Your mind may attach negativity to a neutral event, which negativity influences your state of mind and your mood. Alternatively, your mind may attach positivity to a neutral event, which positively influences your state of mind and your mood. Therefore, positive as well as negative experiences are all self-created. When they are self-created, they can be changed, modified and controlled by yourself. And therein lies the secret to achieving your state of deep inner peace and tranquillity.

Controlling and disciplining the mind is therefore most important. The main source for happiness is in our mind. When your Mind State is one of deep inner peace and tranquillity, you will remain undisturbed and happy, even when the whole environment around you is hostile.

How do you become the master of our own mind? There are 24 hours in a day, and although your subconscious mind works 24/7, your conscious mind does not. You need your conscious mind to reprogram your subconscious mind. Each awaking day you have a continuous flow of many different thoughts, sometimes of longer duration, sometimes just popping in and out of your mind. Mind control makes it possible for you to channel the thoughts that go through your mind and concentrate on those thoughts that help you achieve your goals in life. Since negative thoughts don't provide a contribution to reach your life's goals, you can observe them coming into existence in your mind, and subsequently immediately discard them. This creates space in your mind that you can keep filled with positive thoughts. When your mind is full with positive thoughts, there is no space for negative thoughts to arise and linger.

Popular expressions are: "you are what you think about all day" and "as within, so without". These are rooted in the law of attraction, the law of cause and effect. It is this law of attraction that causes you to attract whatever you focus your energy on. If you focus your mind on what you don't want, you are unintentionally drawing that into your life. For example, if you constantly think about what is stressing you, you'll actually draw more of those situations (and accompanying stressed feelings) into your life. Instead, when you focus on what you do want in your life, you will intentionally attract more of that to come into your life. It goes even further to say that if you focus your attention on achieving a goal and believe not only that you can do it, but that you already have done it, you can achieve virtually any goal you set your mind to. The law of attraction works neutrally, that means in positive as well as negative ways, whether you believe in it or not. Using the law of attraction to your own benefit means thinking only positive thoughts that help you achieve your life's goals. Negative thoughts will always bring about negative actions, which will bring about suffering for yourself and other people, whereas positive thoughts will always lead to positive actions, which in their turn will always bring happiness to yourself and other people. This is all possible through a disciplined, focused and trained mind.

Consider the following guidelines for seizing control of your mind and for changing your mind from a negative state to a positive state to induce happiness:

- accept yourself for who you are. In case you are not satisfied with certain aspects, set a clear goal and work on conscious improvements, but never criticise yourself, rather identify opportunities for improving yourself
- accept that there are certain external circumstances and events over which you have no control (Karma or Fate). Stop resisting things which you can't change
- be satisfied: don't complain or listen to complaints of other people
- be grateful: every day express gratitude and be thankful for everything positive in your life
- meditate: every day set aside time to seek silence, repeat your positive affirmations/mantras and become one with your goals and environment
- remove all self-limiting behaviours and beliefs: fears and limitations only exist in your mind

- think about what you want; don't think about what you don't want
- use visualisation in pictures, your vision board and this Happiness Portfolio to expedite the achievement of your goals
- have only positive thoughts; observe negative thoughts when they arise, but don't give them attention and eliminate them immediately
- focus on all good in your life and think of the ways to make it even better; look for positive aspects in each event, even when at first glance your mind interprets it as a negative event
- reflect on yourself: consciously observe your own thoughts, feelings and actions and correct if needed
- don't be concerned with judgment of others, don't measure yourself against others: think about your own dream, follow your own heart and consciousness
- erase the habit of worrying: worries are self-imposed fears, and thus a self-imposed limitation by the mind
- stop judging events as negative: in nature events just happen and only your thinking makes them negative; they are learning opportunities, and even a negative event has positive aspects. Seek those positive aspects, as everything happens for a reason. Find those positive reasons
- be forgiving: leave emotional baggage in the past, don't drag it to the present
- be balanced: your state of mindfulness that is not disturbed by your or other's emotions, events or circumstances

Mindfulness means observing the External Conditions (reality) as they are, free from emotions and judgement. It means accepting what Karma/Fate brings your way. Controlling your mind does not mean that you emotionally close yourself off from the environment around you, rather it means that you regulate your emotional responses to external conditions as they arise. It means that you have the appropriate emotional processing of those external influences, which processing should be done in conjunction with the aspects of the "deep love and care" goals of your Spiritual State (see Chapter 5).

Live in the Moment

To live in the moment is the second key element which will bring about a deep inner peace and tranquillity. When you look back on your life, can you identify special moments of joy and happiness? For example, when you were celebrating the birthday of your children, when you picked up your new car from the dealership, when you signed your new employment contract, etc. Did you make the most out of those moments? Many such joyful moments occur for only a short period of time and are often only short lived in the mind. They might have seemed like fleeting moments of happiness, which did not linger for long. They did not linger for long, because during such moments, the mind might not have been present, but was already focussing on the next thought, which was far from the special moment. The mind did not live in the moment. The body was there, but the mind might have been somewhere else.

Life happens in the present, not in the past, nor in the future. A good rule is to learn from the past, live in the present, and plan for the future. But don't live in the past, as it is water under the bridge; it can't be changed anymore. Don't live in the future either, because the future never comes; it will always be in the future. The only thing that is real and can be observed by us humans as conscious beings is the present, time in the moment itself. Your life can be compared to one long string of pearls comprising passing moments. When you skip the conscious experience of a moment, you will have skipped one pearl in your life's string. It is like the movie "Click" with Adam Sandler. With a remote that controls time, he skips hours, days, weeks, months and years of his life, to find out that in the end he has not lived at all. Skip too many pearls in the string of your life, and you will feel the same. So try to live in the moment. This is not so easy, but doable, through mind control and mind training:

- enjoy the small daily events in your life, keep chasing the big pleasures, but celebrate the small events with priority
- don't let special moments pass without noticing and enjoying, see divinity in each aspect of your life
- slow down, be conscious of the moment which you are in
- control your mind, to avoid that your thoughts are somewhere else than in the present moment

Lead a Simple Life

Leading a simple life is the third element contributing to a deep inner peace and tranquillity. Leading a simple life first involves removing what is giving complexity, and cluttering your daily life, causing too many distractions from the really important goals of your life. It may involve reducing your Wants (Desires) to your Needs and getting rid of material items that don't add to your level of happiness. Emptying out your basement or garage, and selling or disposing of all long non-used materials and equipment, often generates a feeling of relief. It results in simplicity by creating transparency and focus on what is left. Leading a simple life means finding harmony in your day-to-day activities, and a balance between the four main sources of happiness as presented in the Happiness Portfolio. Try to focus only on priorities, those activities that are truly meaningful for the advancement towards your goals. Finally, it is extremely rewarding when planning your time ahead, when you consciously steer your activities to prevent that circumstances steer you in an uncontrolled way.

Leading a simple life also has an emotional element. It means leaving the past behind you, accepting who you are and how you look, stop resisting things which you can't change, stop worrying and look at events in your life in a neutral way, without any judgement.

Examples of Special Achievement

Clearly recognisable examples of people who have a deep inner peace and tranquillity are:

- Dalai Lama: as figurehead for Tibetan Buddhism, he exerts an aura of tranquillity, peace, spiritual stability, happiness and harmony. He has written many books, conducts regular teachings and promotes meditation, so that other people may attain such happiness from a tranquil mind as well.
- Master Shifu: the small red Panda from the Cartoons "Kung Fu Panda", who trains other animals in the art of Kung Fu. He carries an aura of serenity and peace, assigning Po Ping to find his inner peace as well (in the second movie).

- Jetsun Tenzin Palmo: she is a Buddhist nun, who spent 12 years meditating in a cave in the Himalayas of Northern India.

These are of course extreme examples of people achieving this high level of deep inner peace and tranquillity. Let them serve as a source of inspiration, while you ponder about your own Goals and Actions for achieving happiness from your Mind State.

Applying the Universal Happiness Formula

Happiness =   Baseline Coefficient +   (Current External Conditions > (Needs + Desires + Beliefs)) +   (Goals + Actions + Karma)

The first element generating happiness from your Mind State is the level of your Baseline Coefficient. A high baseline would mean that you already possess a certain level of inner peace and that you don't get upset too quickly about events that effect your life in a negative sense. A low baseline would mean that you are very quickly upset by the smallest disturbance in your life. Increasing your baseline is not easy, as this relates to behavioural patterns set in your character.

The next element of happiness will be generated by your Desires, which fuel Goal setting and Actions to achieving those Goals. Determine your desire for your Mind State, and derive your goals and actions from there. The goal for simplifying your life is probably easiest to achieve, whereas your mindfulness is most difficult to attain. In case your desire for inner peace is significantly higher than your present status, you will have to close a gap. Meditation and consciously contemplating the actions will, however, get you close to your goal.

In contrast to your Material State, your Mind State is fully under your own control.

Your Mind State Happiness Portfolio

It is no coincidence that all three examples of special achievement relate to Buddhism. Happiness from your Mind State, the elimination of emotional suffering, is at the heart of Buddhism. The Happiness Portfolio for your Mind State, therefore, closely follows the Buddhist guidance for deep inner peace and tranquillity:

happiness from	Example Goals	Present status	Example activities to achieve goals
YOUR MIND STATE			
DEEP INNER PEACE AND TRANQUILLITY	Control your mind by dd/mm/yy	to be filled out by YOU	-focus on all good in your life and in every circumstance, stop judging events as negative -be satisfied, be grateful, be forgiving, erase the habit of worrying, think about what you want, don't think about what you don't want, have only positive thoughts -meditate: set aside time for silence, and reflect upon yourself
	Live in the moment by dd/mm/yy	to be filled out by YOU	-enjoy the small daily events in your life -don't let special moments pass without noticing and enjoying, see divinity in each aspect of life -slow down, be conscious of the moment -control your mind, to avoid that your thoughts are somewhere else than in the present moment
	Lead a simple life by dd/mm/yy	to be filled out by YOU	-remove what is giving complexity, eliminate material clutter -reduce your wants to your needs -focus only on priorities, those activities that are truly meaningful for your goal achievement -plan your time ahead, steer your activities, don't let circumstances steer you

Chapter 5

HAPPINESS FROM YOUR SPIRITUAL STATE

Introduction

The fourth, highest and most difficult to access source of happiness relates to your Spiritual State. This brings together the need for love and belonging, for esteem, for self-actualisation, and for self-transcendence. In essence they relate to leading a purposeful life and positively contributing to the life of other people, from which you can derive your feelings of happiness. These needs are the corner stones of human existence, as they are based on the interdependence we all share with other people. We need other people to survive from an evolutionary point of view.

Self-Actualisation

Self-Actualisation is about finding your life's goal, finding your passion in life and pursuing that. At this level, the passion should relate to a cause greater than oneself. It should be for the benefit of others, so the question becomes, how to generate a lasting positive impact on the life of others. The question is easily posed, but the answer might be difficult to find and the answer might shift during your lifetime. Usually a person goes through several stages during their life. At present you are most likely in one of the

following stages: being educated in your early years, developing your career, raising and taking care of your family, maturing in your career, or retiring in your late years. During each of these stages, you are following specific stage-related objectives, which fulfil the purpose of your life in that specific stage. Your transition from one stage to the next stage is the ideal time to reassess the purpose of your life.
When you find such purpose, your life will become much easier and far more rewarding. It will probably need risk taking to get out of your comfort zone and identify your true purpose in life. But when you wake up every morning full of energy and exhilaration, then you know that you are on the right path. The ultimate purpose of life is your contribution to the advancement of others. When you improve the life of others, you elevate your own life at the same time, and enduring happiness will be upon you. The world would be such a better place when everybody would be fulfilling the purpose of their life.

Self-actualisation, finding your passion, living the purpose of your life, are as personal as they can get. You are a unique person, one out of 7.5 billion, and there is no one exactly matching your character and passions. The topic of self-actualisation is analysed in detail in my book *Travel Guide to Self-Actualization*. Please review that book for further guidance on finding your true passion in life. Key activities to achieve your goals can be:

- Create awareness that you have an existing situation that needs to be addressed. Support the development of your awareness by reading relevant books on this topic.
- Take time to find what you really like to do, where your passion in life lies. Link your passion to the improvement of the life of other people.
- Make a structured and thoughtful plan to get from where you are today to living the purpose of your life. Put in sufficient planning efforts and carefully think through your decisions before putting them into action. Support your approach with risk assessments and risk management, and let your analysis show that it is doable.
- Consistently execute your plan, and transform your life, through goals that are detailed, specified, measurable and have a deadline.

The overall aim is to find and live the purpose of your life, your passion, which will automatically lead to the highest level of happiness. It is like the outcome of a mathematical formula: when you live the purpose of your life, your happiness is certain, as it is the only possible outcome. As is often said, live your passion, and you will never work a day in your life.

Examples of Special Achievement

Clearly recognisable examples of people who have achieved Self-Actualisation are:

- Bill Gates: he started Microsoft at a young age and continued to follow his passion for computers and software since then. Later in his career he became a significant philanthropist, donating billions of Dollars to various charities and scientific research. Through both activities he improved the life of other people.
- Bertrand Piccard: he followed the family footsteps in exploring and pioneering. In 2015/2016 he is flying around the world in the first solar-powered airplane, with the aim to lay the foundation for the use of solar-power in new applications. He is putting himself in danger for the greater good.
- Oprah Winfrey: She was born in poverty, but is now a billionaire, from her life-long dedication to Media Communication. Through her talk show, *The Oprah Winfrey Show*, she was able to impact the life of many millions of viewers, as her focus included self-improvement and spirituality.

These are of course extreme examples of people achieving this high level of Self-Actualisation. Let them serve as a source of inspiration, while you ponder about your own Goals and Actions for achieving Self-Actualisation.

Self-Transcendence

Self-Transcendence can be split into two categories: your own behaviour towards other people (internal perspective), and improving the life of other people (external perspective).

During your lifetime you have many relationships with other people. Some relationships are only brief, like at the check-out counter of the supermarket; others are life-long, like with your parents, children and best friends. There are many relationships that are in-between these, such as relationships with work colleagues, neighbours and your sports team. Despite the short, medium or long term nature of your relationships, they all have one thing in common: it is a relationship with another human being. Independent of the duration and nature of your relationships, all human beings long for and expect to be treated similarly.

They expect to be treated with kindness; they expect to be forgiven for mistakes; they expect to be treated with fairness; they expect to be praised when they do something well; they expect to be thanked when doing something positive for you; they expect to be treated with integrity (not lied to, cheated or misled); they expect not to be judged; they expect to be treated with compassion; they expect to be cared for; they expect empathy; they expect tolerance; they expect not to be bossed around; they expect freedom in thinking and expressions; they expect to be free from punishment, etc.

Deep Love and Care for Other People

Translating these expectations back to your own behaviour in relationships with others means showing a deep love and care for other people. The main components of your love and care in your relationships are: kindness, compassion, integrity (behave with honesty and transparency), care, empathy, forgiveness, fairness, tolerance, humility (behave gently and non-judgementally and don't put yourself above another person), praising (don't criticise other people, instead try to understand their point of view, look for the best in other people and praise them), closeness, unselfishness and gratitude. Think about this a bit longer. Isn't this how you would like to be treated in all your relationships as well? When you show deep love and care for other people, this will for certain be returned to you. But don't wait and expect other people to express this behaviour to you first; the initiative for happiness out of this State lies with you (consistent with the law of attraction).

This level of human needs is interpersonal and involves feelings of belongingness. We humans need to feel a sense of belonging and acceptance among our social groups (friends, work colleagues, family, sports club, etc.). Having an intense emotional and physical relationship with another person, having emotional bonds with other people, and investing time to maintain these relationships is often the main contributor to happiness. When you have this, you usually have a strong protection against the impact of events which could throw your life in turmoil.

Because of the nature of Self-Transcendence, the goal of "deep love and care for other people" should principally be the same for all 7.5 billion people in their relationships with other people. Although you may want to adjust the wording of the goal to suit your own style and focus, the inherent behaviour to achieve this goal should principally be unchanged in its nature. You can of course add additional qualities to the elements of relationships, as the above list is not intended to be exhaustive, or you can put a focus on those qualities which result in the highest probability of achieving your goal. In other words, like with all the other elements of the Happiness Portfolio, this may require a certain level of personalisation by you.

Improve the Life of Other People

The highest and external perspective of Self-Transcendence relates to improving the life of other people, by contributing to the advancement of another person on their way to leading a purposeful life. It is this advancement that should result in happiness for that other person. In turn, their advancement should function as a multiplier for improving the life of other people, thus impacting the society at large, as more and more people advance towards the purpose of their life.
The goal of living the purpose of your life (Self-Actualisation) is very closely linked to the the goal of improving the life of other people (Self-Transcendence). Ideally, living the purpose of your life should create a significant benefit for other people. It should unite the advancement of other people with the follow-through on your own passions.

At the level of Self-Transcendence, the goal of "improving the life of other people" should principally be the same for all 7.5 billion people in their relationships with other people. There are, however, many ways in which this goal can be achieved, and generally, these ways will have a direct linkage with the purpose of their life. The result of your analysis of the purpose of your life will feed directly into the activities that you will perform for achieving the goal of helping other people advance in their life. Further activities that you can undertake to improve the life of other people could be: donate a certain percentage of your income to charity; spend a number of hours on voluntary work at the local charity each month;

emotionally and financially support other people with advancing their life, etc.

Similar to the other elements of the Happiness Portfolio, the activities to achieve this goal require personalisation by you. You will attain the highest level of happiness when you unselfishly help other people advance in their life (assuming that you help them advance towards a greater good).

Examples of Special Achievement

Clearly recognisable examples of people who achieved full Self-Transcendence are:

- Mother Teresa: during 50 years she improved the life of the sick, blind, young, aged, disabled, poor and under-privileged people in the slums of Calcutta.
- Mahatma Gandhi: during 50 years he advocated the civil rights of Indians, during his time in South Africa as well as in India, in opposition to the British rule. He advocated non-violence (and did repeated hunger strikes) in achieving independence from the British in his home country.
- Nelson Mandela: during 60 years he defied the racist policies in South Africa in a non-violent way, for which he was imprisoned for 27 years.

These are of course extreme examples of people achieving this high level of unselfishness and dedication to the greater good. Let them serve as a source of inspiration, while you ponder about your own Goals and Actions for achieving Self-Transcendence.

Applying the Universal Happiness Formula

Happiness = Baseline Coefficient + (Current External Conditions > (Needs + Desires + Beliefs)) + (Goals + Actions + Karma)

The first element generating happiness from your Spiritual State is the level of your Baseline Coefficient. A high baseline would mean that you already

derive happiness from your relationships with other people and that you thoroughly enjoy helping other people. A low baseline would mean that interaction with other people does not lead to happiness (or only in a limited way), or perhaps you want to improve your own life rather than focussing on what helps other people.
The next element of happiness will be generated by your Desires, which fuel Goal setting and Actions to achieving those Goals. Determine your desire for your Self-Actualisation and Self-Transcendence, and from there set your goals and take actions.

Your Spiritual State Happiness Portfolio

Improving the life of other people can be achieved within the daily life of your existence, and even the smallest first step, the smallest first contribution, will cause a surge of satisfaction and happiness. Keep pursuing this highest level of happiness and it will surely come to you. It is like the outcome of a mathematical formula: when you consciously and unselfishly improve the life of other people, your happiness is certain, as it is the only possible outcome.

The happiness portfolio for your Spiritual State looks as follows:

happiness from	Example Goals	Present status	Example activities to achieve goals
YOUR SPIRITUAL STATE			
SELF-ACTUALISATION	Live the purpose of your life by dd/mm/yy	to be filled out by YOU	-Create awareness by reading relevant books on this topic -Take time to identify the passion of your life and link it to the improvement of the life of other people -make a structured and thoughtful plan -consistently execute your plan, and measure progress on a periodic basis. Define additional or different actions to close any gaps
SELF-TRANSCENDENCE	Deep love and care for other people by dd/mm/yy	to be filled out by YOU	-treat another person as you would desire to be treated: with non-judgement, loving-kindness and compassion, with integrity -be humble, be gentle, be loving, be praising, don't criticise others, look for the best in other people, spend quality time with your loved ones -take care of the planet Earth and the other Species
	Improve the lives of other people by dd/mm/yy	to be filled out by YOU	-actively live the purpose of your life, assuming its goal is to improve the life of other people -donate a percentage of your income to charity -do voluntary work at the local charity -emotionally and financially support other people with advancing their life

Chapter 6

YOUR COMPLETE HAPPINESS PORTFOLIO

Introduction

What will you do to find enduring happiness? Take the decision to seek happiness in a systematic manner, and do not let your life just develop based on what others do, and your own reactions to others. But perhaps you already found your destiny, your passion and the purpose of your life and you have reached the ultimate happiness level. Perhaps you are already living your dream and are enjoying every moment of it. In that case I can only say: congratulations, you are one of the lucky few, and I hope that you can turn this into enduring happiness.

As with any journey, the travel through life often brings you to new and unknown destinations. What might have been your dream life when you were in your twenties will likely change when you reach your forties, and then again when you reach your sixties. Even your dreams and happiness concepts evolve. What works for you does not necessarily have to work for your another person. As with everything in life, you need to think for yourself and not blindly follow the happiness dreams of others. You are an individual of whom there is only one on this planet, and there will never be another one exactly like you. So follow your own dreams in pursuing happiness. The Universal Happiness Formula and the Happiness Portfolio, however, provide a structured and methodical approach for everyone, irrespective of their personal circumstances, seeking the pathway for enduring happiness.

In today's capitalistic world, many people try to find happiness by improving their material External Conditions, such as receiving a higher salary, driving a bigger car, living in a bigger house, going on a more luxurious vacation, etc. However, since the External Conditions provide only 10% contribution to happiness, this is an extremely inefficient way of achieving/improving happiness. The Happiness Equation shows that the leverage of improving the Internal Expectations is much higher, as these contribute 90%. This means that a person needs 9-times the effort to achieve/improve happiness through the improvement of the External Conditions, then through the improvement of their Internal Expectations. So wouldn't a rational thinking person choose the easiest and shortest path to happiness? A path which is 9 times shorter? The path is also much easier, because Internal Expectations are 100% under their own control, whereas External Conditions are only limited under a person's control. Isn't this an easy and obvious choice?

The Happiness Portfolio and Cycle

The Happiness Portfolio shows how you can find happiness under guidance of a simple analytical and structured process. The connections between the four main sources of happiness become clearly visible in the following chart:

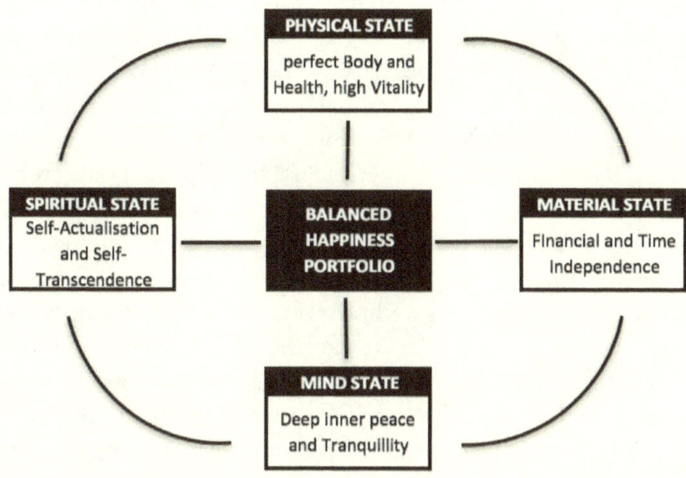

The examples of people that reached an extreme level in either the Physical, Material, Mind or Spiritual State, show that all levels are attainable. The real challenge lies in finding a balance in the achievement of your goals for all four States. It is easy to focus all efforts on achieving happiness from one State, and thereby ignoring the importance of the other States. For example, creating financial independence could be done through stealing, cheating and violence. Think about Bernard Madoff, Enron or El Chapo. Such all-consuming focus on only one of the four States will, however, never lead to enduring and encompassing happiness. As with everything in nature, a moderated balanced approach will lead to success, whereas excesses (to the positive and negative) are rarely sustainable. How are your efforts balanced between the four States?

Even if you lead an ordinary life, with ordinary means, you can derive enduring happiness from setting clear goals for each State, and progressing towards those goals with a certain balance.

Depending on the phase of your life, your goals will have to be adjusted when you transit from one phase to another. So it is advisable not to set an extreme goal that can only be attained in 40 years. Create challenging but achievable goals, work towards them, and once achieved, move your goals to the next level.

For most people, enduring happiness has a few key triggers from the process point of view:

- *Goal setting*: Set goals that are challenging but attainable, as unrealistic goals will lead to frustration of non-achievement, which will lead to unhappiness. The happiness feelings generated by anticipation of reaching a goal usually last much longer than the happiness feeling generated by the goal achievement itself. You could work months or even years to achieve goals, whereas once the goal is achieved, those happy feelings usually quickly return to the baseline level. Revisit your goals regularly, such as once every three months or once a year, or whenever a situation arises that demands a review (e.g. when your life's circumstances change, or when you reach a goal). At each level and State of the Happiness Portfolio, three main components drive the creation of the happiness feelings: the satisfaction arising from the realisation of progress towards achieving the goals, the anticipation of what will happen when you achieve the goals, and the sensation from the awareness that the goals themselves are a cause worth pursuing.
- *Desire*: Goals are based on desires, and desires should be based on passion. Find your passions and live them. Reaffirm and strengthen your desires, your goals and your actions through your daily meditation sessions.
- *Continuous action*: Keep yourself in action to achieve your goals. Actions increase the level of anticipation of reaching a goal. That is why doing nothing rarely makes people happy. Review the effectiveness and efficiency of your actions with a high frequency, e.g. daily or weekly.
- *Diversification*: Spread your actions over multiple goals to ensure variation between the main sources of happiness. When one source dries up, because you have achieved the goal (or the goal is not attainable anymore) and you haven't set a new one yet, the other sources will keep your happiness level elevated. This is why there are 11 elements to the Happiness Portfolio. Diversification is a good risk management principle.

These triggers are visualised in the Happiness Cycle:

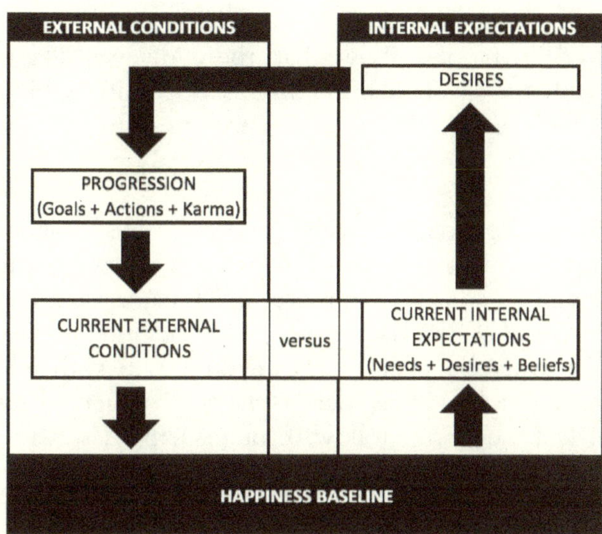

The top three elements of Happiness portfolio are:
First, the largest source of happiness is usually the *Social Interaction*: having an intense emotional and physical relationship with another person, having emotional bonds with other people, and maintaining these relationships.
Second, *Self-Actualisation*: Leading a purposeful life, giving meaning to your life, fuelled by your passion, will elevate your happiness to the highest level, particularly when there is a strong connection to improving the life of other people.
Third, *Deep inner peace and Tranquillity* provides a protection shield against the many influences trying to drag down your happiness level.

Let's turn back to a Buddhist's use of the Happiness Portfolio. A Buddhist would basically remove all desires from the Physical and Material States, but he would keep the desires for the Mind State as well as the Spiritual State. The removal of desire from the first two States results in happiness being achieved when their basic physical needs (food, shelter) and their basic material needs (time to meditate, money to buy food, or even no money at all when they live off offerings) are met. Happiness from these two States should therefore be easy to attain for a Buddhist. The desire in the Mind State is to be free of desires (Attachments) in order to reach a state of deep inner peace and tranquillity. The desire in the Spiritual State is to live the purpose of their life by being a monk (Self-Actualisation) and to show a deep love and care for, and improve the life of other people (Self-Transcendence), through meditation for other humans and teachings.

The above deliberations show that the Universal Happiness Formula combined with the diversified Happiness Portfolio, work consistently for everyone, whatever goals you set for the meaning of your existence on Earth.

The Happiness Portfolio provides concrete and practical guidance to achieve happiness. It guides you through a template portfolio to get you from where you are today to happiness in all major aspects of your life. The Happiness Portfolio, when followed, has the intense power to achieve happiness for everyone, everywhere, anytime. Like with achieving any goal in your life, of course, this needs clarity, courage, determination, and persistence. But when you follow through, happiness will surely come to you, with the certainty of the outcome of a mathematical formula.

Applying the Universal Happiness Formula

Happiness = Baseline Coefficient + (Current External Conditions > (Needs + Desires + Beliefs)) + (Goals + Actions + Karma)

The Universal Happiness Formula can't be applied to your life as a whole, because your life is too complex to be represented in a single formula. You need to apply the formula to each of the constituent elements that have an impact on your happiness level. Here is where the Happiness Portfolio comes in. The Happiness Portfolio breaks your life down into the main sources that drive happiness and make your life's overall happiness level measureable, and therefore manageable. This means that unhappiness in one of the 11 elements of the portfolio does not automatically lead to overall unhappiness, as your diversification on happiness sources will enable you to compensate shortfalls of happiness in one element with surplus of happiness on other elements.

You should also have a longer term perspective on happiness, as expectations in the very short term might be difficult to realise, depending on the time period for which you set your goals and take your actions.

Your Complete Happiness Portfolio

You will have to tweak the Happiness Portfolio to fit your priorities, your stage in life, your purpose of life and your dreams. Use the Happiness Portfolio as your vision board. You may even expand the Portfolio by including pictures that visualise your goals. Support your goal achievement with every proven approach that is available to you, such as visualisation, the law of attraction, etc. Look at the Bibliography reading to learn more about these proven approaches. It is up to you to live your life in a meaningful and purposeful way. Have the courage and willpower to do so and you will find enduring happiness. You already have everything you need to be happy within.

happiness from	Example Goals	Present status	Example activities to achieve goals
YOUR PHYSICAL STATE			
PERFECT BODY	Slim and fit body, xxkg and xx% fat by dd/mm/yy	to be filled out by YOU	-regular physical workouts, like yoga, fitness, walking -healthy diet: low carbs, high protein -no alcohol, no smoking or other substances -regular sun tanning (with protection)
PERFECT HEALTH	Perfect health, free from illnesses by dd/mm/yy	to be filled out by YOU	-enough and deep sleep: don't watch tv/news shortly before going to sleep, program your subconscious mind in a positive way before going to sleep -no eating two hours before sleep -healthy food & drinks: vegetables and fruit; balanced vitamins
HIGH VITALITY	Vital, young looking and feeling by dd/mm/yy	to be filled out by YOU	-sufficient and deep undisturbed sleep -be physically active -keep learning and develop the mind with knowledge. Increase your spiritual wisdom by reading relevant books.

happiness from	Example Goals	Present status	Example activities to achieve goals
YOUR MATERIAL STATE			
FINANCIAL INDEPENDENCE	Have all the money you need to do what you need to do by dd/mm/yy	to be filled out by YOU	-structured and thoughtful long term planning followed by consistent and persistent actions -develop multiple sources of income -control your spending, by spending for the right causes, and be patient -link your financial independence goal to the other elements of the Happiness Portfolio
TIME INDEPENDENCE	Have all the time you need to do what you need to do by dd/mm/yy	to be filled out by YOU	-develop a clear view what you want to achieve with time independence -follow thoughtful and structured actions to realise independence, though these actions can be easily and quickly done -assess the impact of these actions on the other elements of the Portfolio

happiness from	Example Goals	Present status	Example activities to achieve goals
YOUR MIND STATE			
DEEP INNER PEACE AND TRANQUILLITY	Control your mind by dd/mm/yy	to be filled out by YOU	-focus on all good in your life and in every circumstance, stop judging events as negative -be satisfied, be grateful, be forgiving, erase the habit of worrying, think about what you want, don't think about what you don't want, have only positive thoughts -meditate: set aside time for silence, and reflect upon yourself
	Live in the moment by dd/mm/yy	to be filled out by YOU	-enjoy the small daily events in your life -don't let special moments pass without noticing and enjoying, see divinity in each aspect of life -slow down, be conscious of the moment -control your mind, to avoid that your thoughts are somewhere else than in the present moment
	Lead a simple life by dd/mm/yy	to be filled out by YOU	-remove what is giving complexity, eliminate material clutter -reduce your wants to your needs -focus only on priorities, those activities that are truly meaningful for your goal achievement -plan your time ahead, steer your activities, don't let circumstances steer you

happiness from	Example Goals	Present status	Example activities to achieve goals
YOUR SPIRITUAL STATE			
SELF-ACTUALISATION	Live the purpose of your life by dd/mm/yy	to be filled out by YOU	-Create awareness by reading relevant books on this topic -Take time to identify the passion of your life and link it to the improvement of the life of other people -make a structured and thoughtful plan -consistently execute your plan, and measure progress on a periodic basis. Define additional or different actions to close any gaps
SELF-TRANSCENDENCE	Deep love and care for other people by dd/mm/yy	to be filled out by YOU	-treat another person as you would desire to be treated: with non-judgement, loving-kindness and compassion, with integrity -be humble, be gentle, be loving, be praising, don't criticise others, look for the best in other people, spend quality time with your loved ones -take care of the planet Earth and the other Species
	Improve the lives of other people by dd/mm/yy	to be filled out by YOU	-actively live the purpose of your life, assuming its goal is to improve the life of other people -donate a percentage of your income to charity -do voluntary work at the local charity -emotionally and financially support other people with advancing their life

BIBLIOGRAPHY

Byrnes, Rhonda. *The secret*, London: Simon & Schuster, 2006.

Canfield, Jack. *Key to living the law of attraction*, Deerfield Beach: Health Communications, 2007

Canfield, Jack. *The success principles: how to get from where you are to where you want to be*, New York: HarperCollins, 2007

Carnegie, Dale. *How to stop worrying and start living*, New York: Simon & Schuster, 1984

Collier, Robert. *The secret of the ages*, New York: Tarcher/Penguin, 2007

Dalai Lama, *In my own words: an introduction to my teachings and philosophy*, New York: Hay House, 2011.

Dalai Lama & Cutler, Howard, *The art of happiness, a handbook for living*, New York: Riverhead Books, 2003

Haidt, Jonathan. *The Happiness Hypothesis*, London: Random House, 2006

Harari, Yuval Noah. *Sapiens, a brief history of humankind*, London: Vintage, 2011

Hill, Napoleon. *Think and grow rich*, New York: Tarcher/Penguin, 2005

Jones, Dennis Merritt. *Your (re)defining moments–becoming who you were born to be*, New York: Tarcher/Penguin, 2014

Khyentse, Dzongsar Jamyang. *What makes you not a Buddhist*, Boston: Shambhala Publications, 2008

Klein, Stefan. *The science of happiness*, Philadelphia: Da Capo Press, 2006

Lenoir, Frederic. *Happiness-A Philosopher's Guide*, London: Melville House, 2016

Merton, Thomas. *New seeds of contemplation*, New York: New Directions, 2007

Schwartz, David J. *The magic of thinking big*, New York: Simon & Schuster, 2012

Sharma, Robin. *The monk who sold his Ferrari*, London: Thorsons, 1997

ABOUT THE AUTHOR

drs. Hans Beumer is an enthusiastic and seasoned traveller and a passionate Author. He has travelled all over the world, exploring many different cultures.

Throughout his lifetime, Hans has had an energetic drive to accomplish his goals. His personal vision is to make sure that his own goals generate a high added value contribution to the life of other people. He sees it as the purpose of his life to help other people advance with their life. Privately he engages in philanthropy and supports under-privileged children in India to advance to a meaningful life through education and a healthy and secure learning environment.

As an Author he shares his experiences with the world. His books are the carrying vehicles of his passion, and their publishing enables him to reach and touch the life of many millions of other people on all continents. It is his aim to increase the level of happiness in the world.

Contact information:
Please visit www.hansbeumer.com

www.ingramcontent.com/pod-product-compliance
Lightning Source LLC
LaVergne TN
LVHW050942080826
845145LV00004B/1374

* 9 7 8 3 9 0 6 8 6 1 0 9 8 *